This book belongs to:

....

Name of DAD

....

Name of CHILD

....

Age of Child   Date

You're about to get a taste of the fun on each page of the **Dad Storybooks** read-aloud series.

Get ready to enjoy **"Donuts with Dad"** and **"All in a Dad's Day"** and **"The Fathers Walk"**!

NOTE TO DADS

DID YOU KNOW that when fathers take time to read with their children, it can make a big difference in how well they perform in school?

Research shows that when fathers take an active role in their children's education, the child is more likely to do better academically, to participate in extracurricular activities and to enjoy school.

When children have an involved father, it improves their brain functioning starting as early as six months! You can never start too early.

So dads, please enjoy doing these activities with your child, and remember – **reading to your child is a great way to create a lasting bond!**

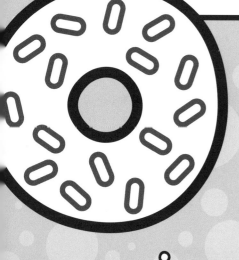

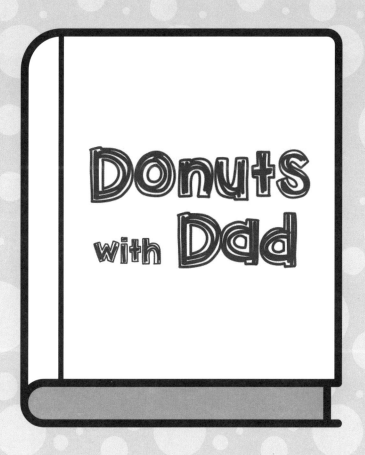

"**Donuts With Dad**" is a book about a delightfully delicious outing between a father and daughter. Any dad will enjoy sharing this imaginative adventure with his child.

Written by **Margaret Bernstein** and illustrated by **Lincoln Adams**, the story showcases a father getting his daughter ready for **"Donuts with Dad"** at school, and planning afterschool surprises including a trip to her favorite restaurant and the park.

Sprinkled with daddy swagger, it's sure to spark many lively read-alouds as fathers boast of their skills, from hairstyling to basketball. Parent and child can use the story as a takeoff point, to plan and enjoy their own special day together.

Ready, Set, COLOR!

I brought the things that a princess should have. Now that's what I call doing Donuts with Dad.

Donuts with Dad

DADS, color this page!

Ready, Set, COLOR!

Donuts with Dad

KIDS, color this page!

DECORATE YOUR DONUT!

Color in your favorite donut flavors in the outlines below.

DECORATE YOUR DONUT!

If you could decorate your favorite donut,
how would you do it? Circle your favorites!

DAD
My favorite toppings are...

Blue Icing

Pink Icing

Green Icing

White Icing

Vanilla Glaze

Chocolate Frosting

Strawberry Frosting

Vanilla Frosting

Oreos

Chocolate Chips

Rainbow Sprinkles

Heart-Shaped
Sprinkles

Other:

CHILD
My favorite toppings are...

Blue Icing

Pink Icing

Green Icing

White Icing

Vanilla Glaze

Chocolate Frosting

Strawberry Frosting

Vanilla Frosting

Oreos

Chocolate Chips

Rainbow Sprinkles

Heart-Shaped
Sprinkles

Other:

"**Donuts with Dad**" is a book about a father and daughter who have an exciting day together.

They start out by attending breakfast at school, and go on to have more adventures including visiting a restaurant and playing basketball.

COLOR ME!

Donuts with Dad

And when that's over,
we'll go out and play.
I brought extra clothes
to top off this day.

Dads and kids, what is your favorite restaurant to visit together?

....

Dads and kids, what sports do you like to play?

....

QUIZ FOR KIDS!

What is your favorite book to read with your father?

....

What is one word that describes your dad?

....

Where is your favorite place to go with your Dad?

....

If you could spend a whole day having adventures with your Dad, what would you two be doing?

....

....

What is your favorite memory with your dad?
What did you do together?

....

....

NOW COMPARE YOUR ANSWERS!

QUIZ FOR DADS!

What is your favorite book to read with your child?

....

What is one word that describes your child?

....

Where is your favorite place to go with your child?

....

If you could spend a whole day having adventures with your child, what would you two be doing?

....

....

What is your favorite memory with your child?
What did you do together?

....

....

NOW COMPARE YOUR ANSWERS!

ADD COLOR TO THIS SPECIAL DAY!

WORD UNSCRAMBLE

It's time to get ready to go to school for Donuts with Dad Day! **Take a look around this room** and unscramble the names of what you see.

CIRHA _ _ _ _ _

RTAEFH _ _ _ _ _ _

DWWION _ _ _ _ _ _ _

AMPSAJA _ _ _ _ _ _ _

UHRETDAG _ _ _ _ _ _ _ _

ADD _ _ _

PLAM _ _ _ _

SUBHR _ _ _ _ _

*Answers on page 35

Ideas for Conversations

Every day, fathers have an opportunity to speak life and pour love into their children. Dads, here are sample conversation prompts, provided by **Books for Bruises Founder Louis Fields Jr.**, that will help your child learn to communicate feelings -- an important life skill.

When you're driving in the car with your child, ask him or her about where they like to go with you.

Example Dialogue:

Dad: "I love when we go to the zoo together. Remember the monkey that made faces?"

Child: "Haha yeah! He looked like Uncle Joe!"

Dad: "He really did! What's your favorite place to go with me?"

Child: "Umm... the trampoline park!"

Dad: "That's a good one. We should go again soon, huh?"

Child: "Yes, and this time I wanna do a flip!"

While flipping through the pictures on your phone or an old photo album, talk to your child about what he or she was like when they were a baby.

Example Dialogue:

Dad: "When you were a baby, you used to laugh so hard when I made silly sounds. You had the cutest little feet too."

Child: "Did I cry a lot?"

Dad: "Only when you were hungry. You loved your bottle."

Child: "What was my first word?"

Dad: "It was 'dada!' And I was so happy I almost cried."

After a school event, sports game or homework session, discuss what makes you proud of your child.

Example Dialogue:

Dad: "I saw how hard you tried today. Wanna know something? I'm really proud of how you kept going, even when that math was tough."

Child: "It was hard... but I didn't give up!"

Dad: "That's what made me proud. You kept trying. That's a big deal."

Child: "Thanks, Dad."

Dad: "Anytime. You're stronger than you know."

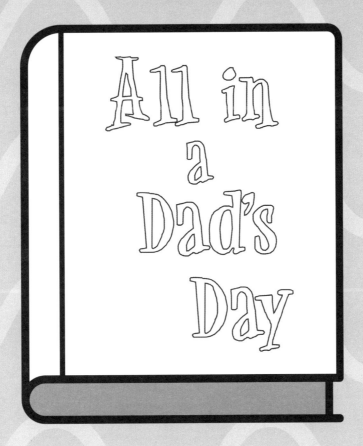

"All in a Dad's Day" is the book that launched the popular **"Dad Storybooks"** series.

This fun-to-read story describes the beautiful memories that a father and son make while going to the park, enjoying a ballgame and just hanging out together.

Written by author/journalist **Margaret Bernstein** and engagingly illustrated by **Lincoln Adams**, it's a satisfying and simple book that casts Dad as his child's protector and hero.

Ready, Set, COLOR!

And what if my only wish, Dad,
was to go to a big game with you?
Then I'd save my money
and stack it up,
to make your dream come true.

All in a Dad's Day

BEST DAY EVER!

DADS
Draw a picture of a fun day out with your **child** here!

KIDS
Draw a picture of a fun day out with your **Dad** here!

IT'S DINNERTIME!

COLOR ME!

All in a Dad's Day

Kids, what's your favorite meal that Dad cooks?

....

Dads, what's your favorite thing to cook?

....

MATCH THE RHYMES

Did you know that all the books in the
Dad Storybooks series are written in rhyme?
Below, draw a line to connect the two words that rhyme.
(The first match is already done for you!)

FALL	SIDE
DO	FED
TIDE	YOU
SEE	DARK
BED	WILD
SHOP	ME
PARK	DROP
CHILD	BALL

*Answers on page 35

COLORING FUN!

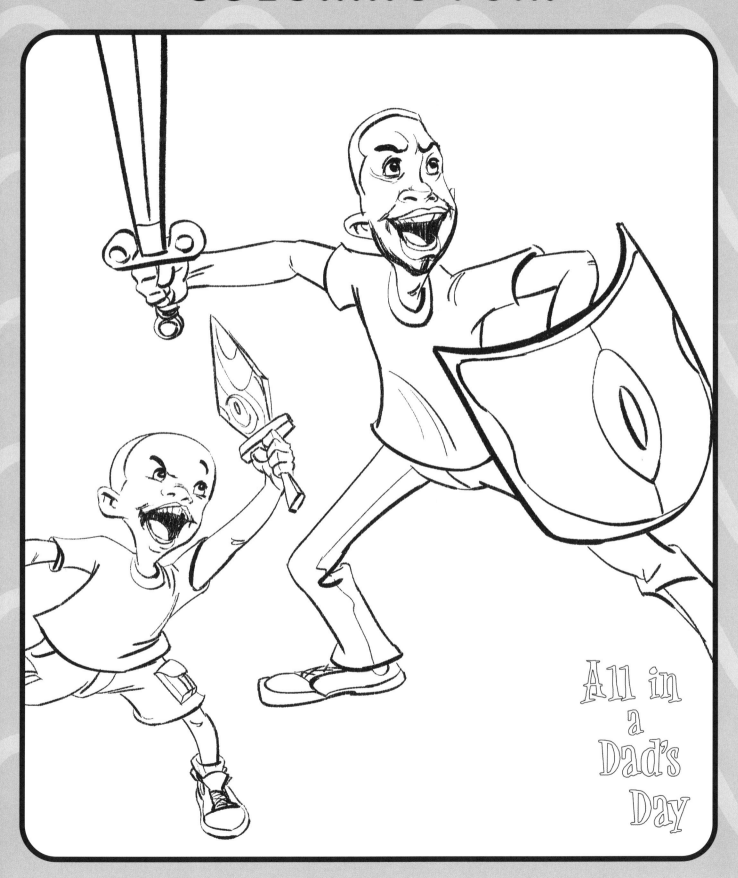

All in a Dad's Day

LEARN SPANISH!

circus = circo

elephant = elefante

¡APRENDER ESPAÑOL!

THINGS TO DO WITH DAD

Here are some fun things to do with Dad, pulled from the pages of **"All in a Dad's Day"**. Circle all the words that you see from the word list.

```
V  S  K  I  T  C  Y  P  A  I  N  T
G  O  L  F  B  S  A  Q  T  E  N  G
D  O  I  U  M  D  G  S  B  L  S  W
C  I  C  O  O  K  F  H  H  B  L  I
B  S  N  M  I  E  G  A  R  D  E  N
F  D  H  I  M  N  D  E  Y  T  L  S
D  A  N  C  E  N  G  L  A  H  B  W
B  N  T  E  N  G  O  R  D  P  O  I
I  C  O  C  O  A  L  E  G  L  A  M
K  E  T  A  I  M  F  A  O  A  N  F
E  F  D  M  E  E  R  D  T  Y  M  D
N  F  I  P  E  S  B  O  W  L  H  T
```

BIKE	**BOWL**	**CAMP**
COOK	**DANCE**	**GAMES**
GARDEN	**GOLF**	**PAINT**
PLAY	**READ**	**SWIM**

*Answers on page 35

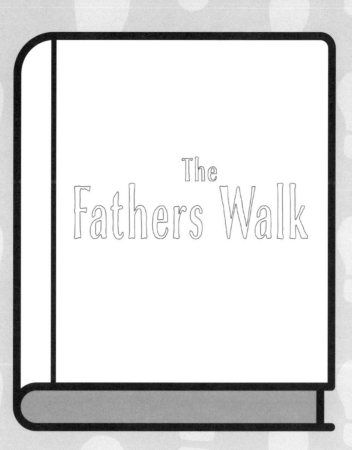

The Fathers Walk

The third book in **Margaret Bernstein's** series of read-aloud storybooks is a tribute to the annual **Fathers Walk**, held at schools across the nation.

It's a feel-good story that conveys the excitement of this annual day when dads and father figures walk hand-in-hand with their children to school. There, they meet their child's teacher, admire the student artwork and even offer to put on a talent show! The fathers promise to come back to volunteer and say they'll remain involved with the school throughout the year.

Illustrated beautifully by **Peyton Leatherman**, the book has become a treasured keepsake of a special day for dads and kids.

Ready, Set, COLOR!

You know what day is really cool?
The day that fathers go to school.

The
Fathers Walk

HELP THEM GET TO SCHOOL!

Can you help them arrive in time for **The Fathers Walk?**

START

END

*Answers on page 35

WHAT DOESN'T BELONG?

Each row contains words that you might see
at a school during **The Fathers Walk** –
BUT one word doesn't belong. Draw a circle around
the word that doesn't belong in the row.

| Classroom | School | Fathers Walk | Monsters |

| Barber | Applesauce | Chef | Salesman |

| Elephant | Pencils | Notebooks | Crayons |

| Donuts | Coffee | Orange Juice | Airplane |

*Answers on page 35

SCHOOL QUIZ
FOR CHILD

What is the name of your teacher?

....

What is your favorite class?

....

What is the name of your school?

....

What is your favorite sport?

....

What is your favorite lunch to eat at school?

....

What do you want to be when you grow up?

....

NOW SHARE YOUR ANSWERS!

SCHOOL MEMORIES
FOR DAD

Who was your best friend in elementary school?

....

What was your favorite sport to play when you were in school?

....

What was your favorite subject when you were in school?

....

What was your favorite hobby when you were your child's age?

....

What is something you would like to teach your child?

....

What is your biggest dream for your child?

....

NOW SHARE YOUR ANSWERS!

COLORING FUN!

We've got dads who come in every size, dads in work boots, dads in bow ties.

The Fathers Walk

How The Fathers Walk Got Started

COLOR ME!

The annual **"Fathers Walk"** goes by many names, including "The Million Father March" and "Dads, Take Your Child to School Day". The event was introduced in 2004 by the **Black Star Project of Chicago**. It's a day when dads, grandfathers, uncles and father figures escort their children to school and pledge to remain involved for the school year. The idea caught on nationally and is now held at thousands of schools. For more information about the walk, contact Fathers Incorporated at:
fathersincorporated.com/million-fathers-march/

The Fathers Walk Pledge

I am responsible for the education of my child.

I will encourage all children to do their best every day at school.

I will speak to my child about the value of learning and the importance of reaching your potential.

I will help with school work and review assignments for completion.

I will praise my child when he/she does well in school.

I will speak with my child's teachers and support them in educating my child.

I will teach my child the value of education and the value of family.

I will work with my child's mother or guardian to achieve the best academic and social outcomes for my child even if I do not live with my child.

© Theresa Mejia Johnson, I Am a Dream, 2012

ANSWERS TO PUZZLES

Word Unscramble, Page 13

C I R H A = chair
R T A E F H = father
A M P S A J A = pajamas
P L A M = lamp
A D D = dad
S U B H R = brush
D W W I O N = window
U H R E T D A G = daughter

Match the Rhymes, Page 20

Fall, ball
Do, you
Tide, side
See, me
Bed, fed
Shop, drop
Park, dark
Child, wild

Word Search, Page 24

```
V  S  K  I  T  C  Y  P  A  I  N  T
G  O  L  F  B  S  A  Q  T  E  N  G
D  O  I  U  M  D  G  S  B  L  S  W
C  I  C  O  O  K  F  H  H  B  L  I
B  S  N  M  I  E  G  A  R  D  E  N
F  D  H  I  M  N  D  E  Y  T  L  S
D  A  N  C  E  N  G  L  A  H  B  W
B  N  T  E  N  G  O  R  D  P  O  I
I  C  O  C  O  A  L  E  G  L  A  M
K  E  T  A  I  M  F  A  O  A  N  F
E  F  D  M  E  E  R  D  T  Y  M  D
N  F  I  P  E  S  B  O  W  L  H  T
```

BIKE	BOWL	CAMP
COOK	DANCE	GAMES
GARDEN	GOLF	PAINT
PLAY	READ	SWIM

Maze, Page 28

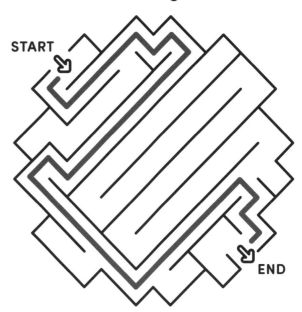

START

END

What Doesn't Belong, Page 29

Row 1: Monsters
Row 2: Applesauce
Row 3: Elephant
Row 4: Airplane

Five Reasons Dads Should Read Regularly With Their Kids

1. **Studies show: Dads make storytime fun.** You guys are good at this! You come up with silly voices and other tricks to make reading time memorable, and that helps your kids realize that reading can be fun.

2. **Being a role model of reading will have lasting results.** Dads, your kids are watching and they want to copy your habits. So let them see you reading in your everyday life. You don't have to always read books. Try reading newspapers, magazines, street signs, maps, computer games.

3. **Everybody gets smarter when their fathers are readers.** Dads, when you spend time reading with their children, they have higher IQs and it improves their social skills.

4. **Boys especially benefit from reading with Dad.** Generally, boys lag behind girls in school achievement. Research indicates that the lack of male role models who are involved in literacy activities could be part of the reason for this. Dads, you're the secret weapon in closing this achievement gap.

5. **Everybody de-stresses when you read aloud.** Research shows that reading is an effective way to overcome stress. Muscle tension releases and your heart rate drops within six minutes of turning pages.

About Dad Storybooks

Great dads deserve great books! That's why we created **Dad Storybooks** – to showcase all the devoted dads who are their child's hero and protector, through compelling stories and multicultural images. Our books, designed to be read aloud, help fathers create a regular ritual of reading with their children. The Dad Storybooks series is sparking a movement of dads who are proudly reading with their kids, on social media and in real life.

If you would like to learn more, follow **@DadStorybooks** on Instagram or Facebook, or go to **www.margaretbernstein.org**